HOW TO MAKE AFFIRMATIONS WORK FOR YOU

ISBN: 978-978-59964-4-9

Published in Nigeria by WORITAL GLOBAL, 2023
6b Lanre Awolokun Street, Gbagada Phase 2, Lagos, Nigeria.
WORITAL (hello@worital.com)
+2348114027024

Cover Design, Interior Layout, Print and Bound by:
WORITAL (hello@worital.com)

FOREWORD

This is not just another book about mere affirmations. It is a book about explaining the power and importance of positive affirmations.

I am a believer in affirmations because I believe the best way to predict the future is to create it. And the purpose of words isn't speaking; The purpose of your words is creation. Human beings have created war and peace by their words over the years. Therefore, I believe that one of the ways to create a family that works is through the power of affirmation and Esther Ijewere has taken us on a powerful journey to see the positivity that affirmations could bring into our lives and how to use that power to our advantage.

I've always had my own share of the blessings positive affirmations could bring , and I've been blessed to share many of them with my family. So , when Esther Ijewere told me about her book , I understood the power and I knew she had to share her knowledge with the world. Every day we see people doing great things in the world and we wonder what they are doing differently besides working hard. It is the power of positive words and affirmations that makes that difference.

My son was preparing to take a major entrance exam into a special talent school a few years ago, but he didn't feel confident enough and we knew that battles are first won in the mind. We watched him initiate a conqueror's strategy- affirmations. He simply created his affirmations, and he repeated it to himself daily till the day he went in for the exams. We weren't surprised that his results were mind-blowing.

Esther Ijewere's book explains and analyzes how to make affirmations work in your daily life, business and relationships. I remember sitting with my wife before we even got married; we had a conversation on how to create the family we want to see. We agreed on our affirmations in the early days. This act of agreement is the most important part of affirmations. The moment couples and families discover the power of affirmations they will normalize the ability to create heaven within their family as against hell.

How To Make Affirmations Work For You By Esther Ijewere gives you an insight on how the words in our affirmation could become a reality and even shape your future.

- Praise Fowowe
Family Therapist

CONTENTS

Authors Note..*xi*

Part 1: Physical health and Emotional well-being..................1
Part 2: Relationships...15
Part 3: Money And Finances................................25
Part 4: How Affirmation Helped Me....................37

Afterward.. 49
Prescription..51

Author's Note

HEALED BY AFFIRMATIONS.

In 2021, I was ill for several months, a period that tested my faith and level of positivity. I almost gave up on myself at a point since my health was not improving. I challenged myself to search for my light again.

I was in between suppressing my emotions just to stay grounded.

I was struggling with balancing my duty as a parent, working, home-schooling my daughters, and staying on top of things. I would speak with folks and act "normal" even when I was falling apart, drained and numb.

I was encouraging people to stay positive, and telling them to keep the faith and keep pushing, yet I was dealing with my physical pain that almost made me relapse into depression.

However, I chose to focus on my light and higher purpose and I found comfort in daily affirmations and prayers. It became a part of me and a routine that changed my life and mindset.

I started by writing down 21 affirmations and read them out daily for 3 months. I saw changes almost immediately, first, my mind shifted positively, then I felt more relaxed, anxiety disappeared, and insomnia left. I became conscious of the words I said to myself and more in tune with my thought process.

I also stopped repressing my emotions and started expressing myself from a place of mindfulness. It evolved into meditation. Being still and releasing negative thoughts.

It was like magic. I never knew that affirmations are life. It dawned on me that as we feed our body with food and nourish it with water as well as everything it needs, the soul needs even more nourishing and nurturing.

It was not my body that was sick. It was my soul. My soul was in dire need of some watering. It had run empty over time, but because it does not function like the body which sends an alarm like a hunger pang and such, we tend to completely ignore every warning sign, until we run out. My soul had run out of energy supply and was sending me signs through my frustrations, fatigue and disinterest in things that ordinarily brought me happiness.

I want to show you that affirmations are not mere words. We should declare and make our confessions without a doubt. Words are powerful. Words are life. They have the power to transform, heal, fix, restore, inspire, and elevate.

Part One

PHYSICAL HEALTH AND EMOTIONAL WELL-BEING

There is a connection between physical health and emotional well-being. Emotional health problems directly affect physical health. If you work in a toxic work environment, soon you will lose the joy and interest you once had, in your job. It will show in the way you carry yourself, do things and engage with others.

This is because your mind and body are deeply connected.

The mind sends signals to the body.

We often prioritise physical well-being over emotional well-being because the wounds reflect differently. However, it is easier to treat a physical injury than an emotional one.

Affirmations are crucial for fighting the invisible battles of the mind, to ensure a healthy mind as well as a healthy body.

Positive confessions used repeatedly, dispel negative energy.

Health affirmations are better said aloud and in the present tense.

You can say it out loud to yourself in front of a mirror or even while meditating.

It feeds the mind and rejuvenates the soul and body.

HEALTH AFFIRMATIONS:

- My health is restored
- My mind produces peaceful thoughts
- This is my self-awareness phase
- I feel secure
- Exercise does wonders to my breathing and my sleep
- I nourish my body
- I eat right
- I focus on delicious, nourishing foods
- I love my body and invest in its good
- I give my body permission to realign and metamorphose
- I am flexible
- I choose the better way: to forgive and to let go

- Healing is available to me
- I will seek help and accept help when offered
- I am grateful for each day and the breath I take
- I get stronger every day
- I heal on the inside and on the outside
- I give love and receive love
- I heal from broken memories
- I receive a state of mind that sees and believes in possibilities
- I hear the heart of God
- I unclothe from every limiting belief and doubt
- I am of sound mind
- I shut down negative voices
- I receive strength for my spirit
- I demolish the spirit of small-mindedness
- I elevate to perfection in my body, spirit and mind

1. SELF CONFIDENCE

Here are some examples of the best positive affirmations for confidence. As you increase your confidence, lose those negative beliefs and focus more on positive thoughts you will learn to start believing in yourself more. You will also develop more room for happiness and success. Let's use these powerful self-love affirmations to remove self-doubt and exude confidence each day.

AFFIRMATIONS FOR SELF-CONFIDENCE:

- I am confident in my abilities and talents
- I trust my instincts
- I am capable of achieving my goals
- I am worthy of love and acceptance
- I embrace my flaws and imperfections
- I deserve to be happy and successful
- I am enough just as I am
- I am capable of conquering any challenge
- My past do not define me; I define myself
- Each day, I am becoming more and more confident
- I am capable of creating the dream life I want
- My mistakes do not make me a failure; they are opportunities for growth
- I forgive myself for all my past failures and move forward with confidence
- I am surrounded by love and support
- I am strong and capable
- I deserve love and success
- I am capable of setting boundaries
- I am proud of who I am

- I choose to see the good in myself and others
- I let go of fear and doubt
- I am open to new experiences and opportunities
- My self-confidence shines brightly
- I am deserving of all the good that comes my way
- I am confident in my decisions
- I am worthy of love and respect
- My self-confidence grows each day
- I believe in myself
- I am capable of achieving great things
- My inherent worth is not determined by others
- I am confident in my appearance

2: SELF ACCOUNTABILITY:

This is taking responsibility for your words, choices, attitudes, behaviours, and actions. It means admitting that you are responsible for your life, and what becomes of it. It requires you to take responsibility for your problems, successes or failures. It is the acceptance that you do not blame others or make excuses.

Why Should you hold yourself accountable?

Just as you run checks on your businesses, it is crucial to hold one's self accountable to measure growth, become more responsible, initiate personal agency, inspire confidence, and a high level of self-validation in you. But most importantly, it prunes you, little by little until you are refined.

These affirmations will not only help you initiate growth and elevation, they will prune you into a better version of who you are right now.

AFFIRMATIONS FOR SELF-ACCOUNTABILITY:

- I love and water myself with validations and reassurances.
- I will not blame others or give anyone else, my power of choice.
- I take back my power of personal agency, I will not lease, sell or trash my right.
- I am responsible for what happens from and through my story.
- If I do not like how my story reads, I have the power to rewrite it.
- I show up for myself and I live life on my terms.
- I gain clarity about my values and understand how I want to show up in the world.
- I filter my choices and decisions through my values.
- I take back my power to say Yes, to only things I want to say yes to, and No, to things I want to say no to.

- I commit to showing up only as myself and no one else.
- I show up no matter how hard or difficult it is for me.
- I make better and wiser choices.
- I commit to being pruned daily for self-discovery and refinement.

3: VALIDATION:

Validation has become as important as living. It is the recognition a person and their feelings or opinions need from someone, other than themselves.

The desire to have someone else's approval of what you say, do and believe, sounds like a lot of power, handed over to another but it happens every day. We have at one time or the other, sought the validation of someone or people.

Sadly, when we are constantly seeking approval from other people, we are only inviting more anxiety, low self-esteem and fear. We remain stuck in the same pattern.

AFFIRMATIONS FOR VALIDATION:

- I am enough
- I do not wait to be validated before I share my light with the world.
- I show up confidently
- I take constructive criticism and open myself to growth
- I take feedback and turn it into an opportunity to sharpen my talent
- I do not respond to negativity with negativity
- I do not allow unseasoned words to break me
- I filter what I choose to listen to
- I am a work in progress
- Success is not definitive but what we choose to make of it
- Perfection is a mirage
- Excellence is not a destination, but a journey
- I permit myself to enjoy the process
- For in the process lies the glory
- I can start from where I am, as who I am, and with what I have
- I am not afraid of the spotlight
- I will not put my light under a bushel
- I am a city set on a hilltop
- I will not give anyone permission to define me

4: COPING WITH INTENSE FEAR:

This is a distressing emotion triggered by real or imagined threat, danger, pain, evil and other feelings. Intense fear is a paralysing feeling of anxiety or apprehension.

In moments of intense fear, affirmations help you still the ragging billows. It calms the heart and recovers the body from the state of fear.

AFFIRMATIONS TO COPE WITH INTENSE FEAR :

- I am safe.
- I am brave.
- I can move past this moment.
- I am in charge.
- As I breathe, I am calm and relaxed.
- I have survived my anxiety before. I will survive it now.
- My body is my ally.
- My soul, mind and body listen to me
- I speak into my spirit that no worry, distress or agitation stays here.
- I experience tranquillity in my soul and spirit.
- I decree peace in my body.
- I won't be derailed from my destination by fear.

- I overcome and expose every fear to the light.
- Darkness can not stand the light.
- I see light illuminating every trigger of fear in my life .

5: COPING WITH SOCIAL ANXIETY:

Anxiety is worry about events, as simple as ordinary, routine issues. It is characterised by avoidance of social situations emanating from self-consciousness, fear of being judged, fear of being ridiculed, feelings of embarrassment and others.

It could be triggered by past unpleasant events. Here are powerful affirmations to help you get through social anxiety.

AFFIRMATIONS FOR SOCIAL ANXIETY :

- I act with confidence because I know what I am doing.
- I am different and unique, and that is Okay.
- I am safe in the company of others.
- I love and I am loved.
- I am prepared and ready for this situation.
- People assume I can do this, I know I can, and I will.
- I am at ease when talking to other people.
- I am not an imposter, I was created for this

- I am equipped to deliver beyond expectations
- I rise above societal expectations of me
- I focus on enjoying
- It is perfectly alright not to blend in
- I was chosen to do this because I am good at it
- I am in control of my nerves
- I won't lose my train of thought
- Perfection is a mirage, I am here for excellence

6: COPING WITH GRIEF

Grief is a response to loss, it comes with waves of emotions, such as: pain, sadness, fear, desperation, denial, hopelessness and guilt.

AFFIRMATIONS FOR COPING WITH GRIEF :

- I allow myself to feel these waves of emotions
- Everything I am feeling is normal
- I am human and should feel this way
- I won't let guilt rip me apart
- I did the best I could And that is enough
- I commit to healing, today
- I open my heart to gratitude

- I appreciate the memories we shared
- I am channelling my pains into birthing something good
- I use my experience to help others
- I accept help and show gratitude to those who stand by me
- I won't let grief push my loved ones away
- I build supportive friendships
- I live in the moment
- I make each day count
- I won't give grief the power to leave me undone

7: COPING WITH TRAUMA:

Traumatic experiences destroy survivors' self-confidence, self-worth and trust in others. Trauma survivors struggle with the burden of guilt and self-blame.

Trauma is damaging and a tough road to navigate. However, affirmations for trauma help survivors deal with negative emotions, learn self - compassion and fight each day, to pull through.

AFFIRMATIONS FOR COPING WITH TRAUMA:

- I am deserving of love
- I give love and kindness
- I do not let the bad experiences define me
- I am wonderfully made
- I take ownership of my thoughts and emotions
- It is okay to feel overwhelmed, sad, angry and vulnerable
- This is my life and I can't change what has happened
- But I have the power to rewrite my story
- I speak my truth
- I will not be voiceless
- I use my voice to fight for others
- I will not be shamed
- My voice is my weapon of truth and conviction
- Each day, layer by layer, I make consistent progress
- I am healing
- I am transforming
- I turn my bad experience into a powerful gift
- I stand, unafraid
- I am not limited by my experience
- I am not beneath anyone because of the experience
- I deserve equal treatment
- I open my heart to accept and give trust

Part Two
RELATIONSHIPS

R elationships provide us with allies, destiny-partners, purpose-sojourners and beautiful family and friends to share our lives with. No one wants to walk alone. It is too lonely. Relationships change our lives and unlock doors to better, more beautiful and richly rewarding lives.

AFFIRMATIONS FOR RELATIONSHIPS:

- I choose friends that are healthy
- I am committed to being a great support system to my friends
- My family is incredible
- I am my truest self with my family
- I am an amazing person, so I attract amazing friends
- I do not feel the pressure to be anyone else with my friends
- My family loves me unconditionally

- I love my family unconditionally
- I am loved by my family
- I do not attract disloyal friends
- I make friends I can rely on
- I am a reliable friend
- Family is everything
- I show up for my friends and family
- I feel joyful when I spend time with my family
- My family is not perfect but we are giving our best to each other
- I am a supportive and kind spouse
- I love my children unconditionally
- I give my children the best of my time and energy
- Each passing day is an opportunity to serve others
- I light the light of others
- My spouse is my ally and loyal friend
- I receive an abundance of love all around me
- I pay attention to the needs of my children
- I listen to the needs of my spouse
- I speak my spouse's love language
- I am generous to my spouse
- I do not belittle or disrespect my family before anyone
- I enjoy every moment spent with my friends
- My friends are imperfect but it is fine

1: MARRIAGE:

The union of two different personalities, backgrounds and experiences, who vow to love each other and do life together.

Affirmations in marriage help couples to stay focused on the type of marriage they want. It helps them get through difficult times in marriage and strengthens their commitment. Marriage is a lifetime commitment, as such, couples need all the help and goodwill they can get to navigate the journey.

AFFIRMATION FOR MARRIAGE:

- I value my spouse for all they do in our marriage.
- I am passionately in love with my spouse.
- I love my spouse unconditionally.
- I have faith in our marriage.
- Our marriage is a miracle.
- The unconditional love I receive from my spouse makes me a better person.
- My wife/husband and I strive for greatness in our marriage.
- I accept my wife/husband unreservedly.
- My spouse and I are faithful to each other.
- On cloudy days, we will hold each other up.
- Our marriage is filled with laughter and joy.

- We are contented with each other.
- Our bond grows deeper each day.
- We forgive and erase any wrong easily.
- I commit to reigniting the hearth of our home.
- I am full of love and positivity.
- Our marriage will thrive and flourish delightfully.
- We rediscover each other intimately.
- We are proof of a happy, fulfilled and Godly marriage.
- My wife/husband is very supportive and encourages me to go after my dreams.
- I am devoted and committed to my spouse.
- My marriage is my priority.
- I respect my wife/husband's individuality.
- Every day our marriage grows stronger.
- I appreciate and respect our differences.
- I love doing things that make my wife/husband happy.
- I tell my wife/husband that I love them every day.
- I am loved.
- I am okay with my spouse having male/female friends.
- My wife/husband and I make a great team.
- My wife/husband and I are so in love.
- I understand my spouse, and they understand me.
- Our bond is strong. Nothing can separate us.

2: FRIENDSHIPS

Walking the journey of life without a companion is tough. Friendships are powerful, it helps us build connections with other people whose values align with ours, who share similar interests with us and who inspire and motivate us.

Life is uninteresting without friendships. We achieve twice, what would have taken us longer to achieve, because of friendships.

AFFIRMATIONS FOR FRIENDSHIPS :

- I attract destiny alliances
- My journey in life is propelled by loyal allies
- I give and receive positive energy for my journey
- I plug into healthy friendships
- My friendships are focused and goal-oriented
- I multiply in million folds because of my friendships
- I do not invite time-wasters into my life
- I am a blessing to my friendships
- I inspire, support and catalyse my friendships
- I exude peace and joy
- My friendships are blessed because of me
- I love my friends and their imperfections
- I deserve love and healthy friendships

3: PEACE AND LOVE

Peace is the absence of conflict or friction. Peace means tranquillity. Love is a tender personal affection for someone.

Peace and love make life worth living. They are the balm that soothes us from the battering of life.

AFFIRMATIONS FOR PEACE AND LOVE:

- I am peace, I am love, and I share both generously
- I bask in tranquillity in spite of life's many challenges
- I do not lose my peace and calmness
- I speak in measured tone
- I speak words that promote peace
- I speak into my heart and soul that there is no agitation
- I am love personified
- I bear fruits of love
- I experience ease all around me
- My relationships experience peace and love
- I live a life of ease, all year round
- I flourish like the olive tree, planted by the stream
- I am surrounded by the peace which surpasses all understanding
- I will not be shaken
- I will not be moved

- A hedge is around me, my family, my marriage and my relationships
- I decree impenetrable peace
- Wherever I step feet, I leave a fragrance of peace

4: SELF RESPECT:

Staying true to your values and convictions, and refusing to compromise is self-respect. If you respect yourself, you will love and care for yourself. Being convinced that you are worthy, will make you treat yourself just the way you feel. When we show consistently that we have self-respect, we attract people who also respect and treat us right.

AFFIRMATIONS FOR SELF-RESPECT:

- I wholeheartedly love and cherish myself
- I love every inch of my body
- I am a wonder to behold
- I will not compromise my values
- I will treat myself right
- I will not force relationships
- I will let go of anything that is no longer serving me positively

- I will not fight for acceptance.
- I invest in the right relationships
- I say no to people-pleasing
- I pamper, love and care for my body
- I am kind to myself every single moment
- I make and keep my promises to myself
- I put myself first
- I look out for myself

5: BOUNDARIES:

Boundaries define us. It shows ownership. It is that invisible line that shows where one person begins and the other ends. Boundaries point to our parameters and how we can protect them. Boundaries require that we take responsibility for our actions and also help others do the same.

AFFIRMATION FOR BOUNDARIES:

- I exercise my rights to choose what I let in, and what I keep out
- I won't be guilt-tripped into dishonouring my boundaries

- I stand for my values and convictions without disrespecting other people's choices
- My resources are important, so I will protect it
- My personal space is a top priority, I consciously protect it
- I should not get angry if someone says NO to me
- I start and finish my tasks within the agreed timeframe
- Boundaries keep me safe and sane
- I set boundaries in my relationships
- I deserve healthy relationships
- Boundaries ensure my choices are seen
- Boundaries eliminate misunderstanding
- Love shines forth because of boundaries
- I enjoy a wholesome marriage rooted in boundaries
- I am not entitled to anything

6: LEISURES:

This is free time. A time spent away from work, chores, businesses and tasks.

AFFIRMATIONS FOR LEISURES:

- I make time to relax without feeling guilty
- I consciously make time for myself
- Every day, I set time aside for self-care
- No one will take care of me if I don't
- My body deserves to have fun
- Fun is a crucial part of living
- I will not jeopardise my health by working without creating time for leisure
- I enjoy recreational activities that help me to relax

Part Three

MONEY AND FINANCES

Money mantra and confessions are important because our finances impart every other area of our lives. Making better, informed financial decisions determine our quality of life. Abundance and lack exist side by side, the difference is in our choices and decisions.

It all begins with the mind. The mind is the battlefield. It is the place where winning or losing takes place first before it materializes. As far as your mind can see, you will achieve.

What we tell ourselves, becomes our reality.

Affirmations about money don't necessarily reflect your financial status at the moment, it works on your mind, showing and sowing seeds of possibilities.

AFFIRMATIONS FOR MONEY :

- I am wealthy, healthy, and happy.
- Money is flowing into my life.
- I am open to receiving abundance.
- I am creating wealth.
- I am prosperous and prosperous people like me.
- I know that I will always have plenty of money, because it is my natural state of being.
- Money flows to me effortlessly.
- I am generating money on all levels of my life.
- I am deserving of the riches that I desire.
- My income is always increasing.
- Money can't stay away from me.
- I deserve to have all that I need and more.
- Money flows freely to me and through me.
- Money is easy and plentiful for me.
- I am a prosperous and abundant person.
- I always have more than enough money for what I need and want.
- I am a money magnet.
- I have an abundant supply of money.
- Every day, I make more and more money.
- I have a large sum of money in the bank.
- I am a bountiful millionaire.

- Money is a positive tool in my life.
- My relationship with money is healthy.
- Every day I grow richer.
- I have plenty of money to meet my needs.
- I am confident that I will manifest the financial resources I need in the time frame that I need them.
- I am wealthy, healthy, and happy.
- Money is flowing into my life.
- I am open to receiving abundance.
- I am creating wealth.
- I know that I will always have plenty of money, because it is my natural state of being.
- Money flows to me effortlessly.
- I am generating money on all levels of my life.
- I am deserving of the riches that I desire.
- My income is always increasing.
- Money can't stay away from me.

1: BUSINESS:

Business is an economic activity. It is the buying and selling of products. Business is mostly for profit. No one talks about money and finance without mentioning business. People also start a business to meet the needs of society.

AFFIRMATIONS FOR BUSINESS :

- I receive uncommon insights
- I am a partaker of goodness
- Business secrets are revealed to me
- My strategies are mind-blowing
- I sit with kings and kingmakers
- I birth original ideas
- My business flourishes
- Kings and queens shall come to my rising
- I excel beyond human understanding
- My customers are happy with me
- My business deserves every commitment I make
- I press onwards to the global level
- I receive awards and recognition for how I run my business
- I work with a healthy business culture
- I make steady profits
- I manage my business well
- I employ the best employees
- I am a visionary, and I commit to building a lasting brand
- My brand is known in every place
- I satisfy my customers
- I am a wonder to behold

- I build little into abundance
- I am innovative
- I execute fresh, creative and powerful ideas

2: WORK:

Everyone engages in one work or the other. Any activity that requires physical or mental effort to do, is work. This activity is usually done for money. Work can become overwhelming and tough. Affirmations help you cope with moments of confusion, overwhelm and difficult moments. It helps you stay in tune with yourself no matter what you are experiencing.

AFFIRMATIONS FOR WORK :

- My work gives me excitement
- I stay focused on the vision at the moment
- Opportunities abound
- I attract opportunities to my work
- I am grateful for my job
- I am worth every promotion
- I am ready for leadership
- I overcome challenges
- I give my best every day

- My work gives me satisfaction
- My work sorts my bills
- I push every day
- I am a unique blend of gifts

3: CAREER:

This is one's profession, chosen line of work or education. It is not an easy path to navigate. Sometimes, we give our best but things still turn out differently. From finding the right job for your career dreams to getting promoted at your workplace to preparing for interviews and presentations, to dealing with difficult colleagues or a difficult boss.

It takes grit and resilience, and you need a positive mindset to overcome these challenging routes.

AFFIRMATIONS FOR CAREER :

- My career paves way for an incredible future
- I stay calm, collected and reasonable at all times
- I will not let difficult moments cost me future opportunities
- I prioritise my mental health

- I prepare for interviews and ace them
- My colleagues enjoy working with me and they love my presence
- I am open to learning new things every day
- I have all the expertise and skills needed to excel
- I deserve to be promoted
- I am focused on growing and becoming better than I am
- Challenges are a part of life
- I will not let challenges determine how I react, think or execute my tasks
- I have a vision for my job, I am committed to a progressive movement
- I have set goals, and I smash each goal every time
- I rise constantly in my career
- I help my colleagues when they need help
- I remain consistent in seeking knowledge
- I invest in personal development goals
- I stay happy every day at work
- I am happy at my workplace

4: SAVING:

This refers to income put aside for more meaningful use or for later. It is deferred consumption. No matter how many affirmations we recite about our money matters and finances, if we do not make conscious efforts to reduce expenditures, we may be wasting time. Affirmations propel you to dispel negative and hindering tendencies. It works best if there is a balance between confessions and work. Faith without work is useless.

AFFIRMATIONS FOR SAVING :

- Money is naturally and easily attracted to me
- I receive financial freedom
- My money works for me
- I deserve and enjoy financial success
- I am a good money manager
- My money multiplies
- I respect my labour by using money wisely
- I am generous with my money
- I apply wisdom to money
- Opportunities to make more money are open to me
- My money grows in leaps and bounds
- I do not worship money
- Money recognises me and answers when I call
- I am grateful for the money at my disposal
- I am grateful for the money I manage, for it will unlock more.

5: INVESTMENT:

An asset or item acquired with the goal to generate income, building wealth or saving from income is an investment. Investment is the surest way to build generational wealth. It is not enough to save. Saving does not correlate with building wealth, even though it does cushion one from rainy days

AFFIRMATIONS FOR INVESTMENT:

- I delay gratification to invest
- I open my mind to investment teachings
- I commit to learning about my finances
- I enjoy investing
- I reap the rewards of my financial growth
- I enjoy the financial ease that investing releases
- I will pay attention, read and research about new investment opportunities
- I will make my findings and think carefully before any investment decision
- I will not invest in quick, unreasonable means
- I am in control of my emotions
- I look before I leap
- I am optimistic about investments
- I commit to diligently making inquiries and findings before investing

- I make smart and authentic investment decisions
- I seek out good investments
- I cultivate patience in my investments
- I am building generational wealth

6: SPENDING:

This is using out or exhausting money. Some people can't save or invest because of their money habits, such as emotional spending. Impulsive spending habits will cripple even a top earner. In the case of chronic emotional spending, debt and bankruptcy are inevitable. Being in charge of your feelings and emotions is the first step to financial freedom, and affirmations will help you walk through these difficult moments. It will renew your mind as you constantly confess it.

AFFIRMATIONS FOR CONTROLLING SPENDING:

- I make better financial choices
- I buy only what I need
- It is okay to give myself a treat sometimes
- It is okay to spoil myself sometimes

- I won't spend to please anyone
- I won't spend to be accepted
- I won't spend on things that do not matter to me
- I overcome feelings that cause me to become compulsive with spending
- I remove myself from places that put me in debt
- I say NO to the black tax
- I set healthy boundaries around my finances
- I will spend my money wisely
- I will learn financial literacy
- I journey into financial bliss
- I won't be blackmailed into spending unnecessarily
- I receive insight into a path to financial freedom

Bonus

HOW AFFIRMATION HELPED ME

THE 30 "I STATEMENT" AFFIRMATIONS THAT WORKED FOR ME

- I am healed
- I am whole
- I am resilient
- I am a magnet for light and love
- I am winning in life
- I am highly favoured by the divine
- I am at peace
- I have will-power
- I am fine
- I am manifesting a life of ease
- I am manifesting clarity of purpose

- I deserve it all; the beautiful house, the stable income, the happiness, the answered prayers, the love, the global opportunities, the new connections, and the manifestation of my daily affirmation. I deserve every ounce of goodness in this world.
- I am ready to take actions that will make my dreams come true
- I am positioned for greatness
- I will live a long, happy life with people who bring me joy
- I will love more deeply and laugh more freely as time goes on
- I will discover and appreciate new versions of myself, again and again
- I will always be proud of the person that I have grown into
- I welcome abundance of everything good into my life
- I live a life of plenty. I will continue to manifest abundance
- I affirm that my needs and wants are met; I will never lack
- I am a very lucky person. Good things are constantly happening to me
- I am always in the right place at the right time
- I am a magnet for abundance and prosperity

- I can see everything turning around for my good
- I am entering a new phase full of love, peace, divine opportunities, blessings, good energy, positive connections, higher thoughts, and spiritual wellness, I welcome it all right now! I deserve it
- I affirm that every disappointment is turning around for my good
- I am confident that my future will be full of love, expansive growth, global opportunities, and divine favour
- I receive grace and favour in the sight of everyone that matters to my destiny
- I attract wealth and good energy into my life. I deserve to live a life of abundance. I am exactly where I need to be. Everything is working out in my favour

AFFIRMATIONS FOR SPIRITUALITY: EVERYTHING IN LIFE HAPPENS FOR A REASON.

- I am guided by fate but not beholden to it.
- I believe that we are all guided by divine providence.
- I believe in the healing power of the spirit.
- I believe that I can achieve inner peace.

- I know that I exist for a divine purpose.
- I have 100% trust in God's divine plan.
- I know I deserve all the happiness that I receive.
- I believe that my spirit is in harmony with the universe.
- I know that I am a spirit-given flesh.
- The universe will provide anything I need.
- I know that the Holy Spirit flows through me.
- I am a vessel of the divine spirit.
- I know that all of my triumphs are a gift from God.
- All of my hardships are opportunities to become closer to God.
- I believe that God guides me in everything I do.
- I am happy to share my blessings with others.
- I believe that love can heal my soul.
- I know I can achieve a higher state of consciousness with the universe's help.
- I believe that God works through me to help others.
- I know that God has given me the power to help myself.
- I have the power to brighten up the lives of everyone in my life

AFFIRMATIONS FOR GOOD HEALTH

- I radiate positive energy and good health.
- I am active and full of energy.
- I appreciate my body with all its strengths and flaws.
- I deserve good health and a fit body.
- I bless my body every day.
-
- I love being healthy and energetic.
- Every cell of my body is filled with positivity, happiness, and love.
- I am energetic, happy, and wonderful.
- My physical and mental health is in an excellent state.
- I have good health and a fit body now.
- I love my body with all its imperfections.
- I feel invigorated and renewed.
- It is easy to take care of my body.
- I manifest excellent health and a perfect body.
- I heed and accept my body's messages to me.
- I love providing nourishment to my body.
- I feel healthier and fitter every day.
- My soul is stimulated and revitalised.
- I feel strong and healthy.
- I am the creator of my health.
- I am caring and attentive to my body.

- I am at the ideal body weight.
- My body is healthy and strong.
- I make healthy and wholesome choices.
- I choose foods that are most beneficial for my wellness and health.
- My body appreciates how I care for it.
- I feel happier and healthier.
- I am vibrant and alive.
- I am thankful for my healthy and fit body.
- I am feeling great, robust, and lively.
- I am brimming with joy and pride.
- I have a healthy and energetic mind and body.
- My body is positive, energetic, and excited.
- My life is evolving beautifully.
- I am worthy of a healthy body and a happy mind.
- I fully accept my position in life and I am alert to any opportunity to flourish.
- My focus is on progressing in the right direction.
- I am receiving ample love and support during this process.
- I create good health by exploring opportunities and discussing my wellness.

30 DAYS DAILY POSITIVE AFFIRMATIONS TO IMPROVE MOTIVATION

- I trust myself to make the right decision. I have the tools and abilities that I need to do so.
- I am becoming closer to my true self every day. Every challenge, loss, and success brings me closer to that goal.
- I am learning valuable lessons from myself every day, and I will continue to ensure I keep this up.
- I am the architect of my life; I build its foundation and choose its contents.
- Today, I am brimming with energy and overflowing with joy. These are emotions I can use to motivate myself throughout the day.
- My body is healthy, my mind is brilliant and my soul is tranquil. This shall provide me with the alignment I need to conquer the tasks ahead of me today.
- I am superior to negative thoughts and low actions.
- I have been given endless talents and today, I begin to utilise them. I have the confidence to do so.
- I forgive those who have harmed me in the past and peacefully detach from them.
- I allow myself to be who I am without judgment because that is what is going to allow me to be the happiest person in my life.

- I listen to my intuition and trust my inner guide because that is going to take me closer to what makes me truly happy.
- My drive and ambition allow me to achieve my goals because I have a fire inside of me, pushing me forward.
- I possess the qualities needed to be extremely successful and I have the confidence to apply those skills in ways that will enable me succeed.

-

- Creative energy surges through me and leads me to new and brilliant ideas.
- My ability to conquer my challenges is limitless; my potential to succeed is infinite.
- I am courageous, and I stand up for myself and for others who may need my help because it is the right thing to do.
- I wake up today with strength in my heart and clarity in my mind that give me the ability to make good decisions throughout my day
- I am at peace with all that has happened, is happening and will happen.
- I permit myself to do what is right for me because that is how I allow myself to be the most authentic personality that I can be.

- I give myself space to grow and learn because I understand that there is always room for growth in our lives.
- I am blessed with an incredible family and wonderful friends.
- I acknowledge my self-worth and I am willing to improve in areas that I consider are my weaknesses right now.
- Though these times are difficult, they are only a short phase of life. Everything that is happening now is happening for my ultimate good.
- My efforts are being supported by those around me who also want to see me succeed and do amazing things.
- My obstacles are moving out of the way; my path is carved toward greatness. I just need to continue walking on that path.
- I am creatively inspired by the world around me, and I can use that inspiration to achieve amazing things in my life.
- My mind is full of brilliant ideas that I can use to benefit myself and others.
- I put my energy into things that matter to me because that is what brings me the most happiness in my life.

- I am at peace with who I am as a person because I understand what is important to me and what is not and I live by my values.
- I make a difference in the world by simply existing in it and trying to make it a better place in whatever ways I can.

How Long Do Affirmations Take To Work

The time it takes for affirmations to positively impact your self-confidence can vary. It depends on how often you repeat the affirmation and how deeply ingrained the negative thoughts are, that you are trying to change. It is essential to be patient with yourself and trust the process.

Remember, self-confidence takes time and effort to build. It is essential to be kind and patient with yourself as you work on improving your self-confidence. By repeating these affirmations and engaging in positive self-talk, you are taking a step towards a more confident version of yourself. Keep going and trust the process!

When using affirmations, try to make them specific and in the present tense. For example, instead of saying, "I will be confident," try saying, "I am confident." This helps your brain to believe the statement at the moment.

Also, make sure that the affirmations align with your values and beliefs. It won't be effective if you repeat statements that don't feel true to you.

Finally, try to come up with your own affirmations that speak specifically to the areas where you want to improve your self-confidence. Customising them to fit your own needs can make them even more powerful.

Good luck on your journey toward realignment, purpose, clarity, possibilities and elevation.

AFTERWARD

I am so grateful that you got to read this book to this level. This book works like medication. It is not to be taken in all at once. It is yours to unlock for whatever you are dealing with at any moment.

I hope that you patiently apply each affirmation, one day at a time and for the specific challenge or hurdle you need to get past.

Affirmations are deep and effective. I am a witness to its potency. I encourage you to begin with a receptive spirit and a ready heart.

You will see your life take a new turn.

You remain consistent with it and watch how much you will achieve.

I am earnestly praying that your eyes open, and your heart receives and internalises all that have been made available for your transitioning into greater and larger spaces.

PRESCRIPTION

Do not abuse.

Take one day at a time, repeated doses until you feel a connection.

If symptoms persist, refer back to the prescription, and restart treatment.

To cure persistent or acute illness, repeated, higher dosage is advised.

Remember where the attack hits always- your mind. It is a battlefield. Do not begin treatment and stop. You will relapse and it is even more difficult to fight after a relapse. Do not give it a chance. Attack with these arsenals. That is the only way to disarm and nullify the attacks.

I look forward to seeing you at the top, whole and ready to be all that you have been called to be.

I would love to read your review, personally, and connect with you on social media:

FaceBook : Esther Ijewere
Twitter : @Esther Ijewere
Instagram: @estherijewere
Email:ijewereesther@gmail.com
LinkedIn: Esther Ijewere
YouTube :Esther Ijewere

Tag me in all your reviews and I will be on your timeline. It is time to manifest.

Best wishes,

Your partner in realignment,

Esther.

Made in the USA
Middletown, DE
28 June 2023